I0896491

NVIDIA

第一屆
李國鼎獎
第一屆
李國鼎獎

NVIDIA

ODYSSEYS

ERIN SILVER

CREATIVE EDUCATION · CREATIVE PAPERBACKS

Published by Creative Education and Creative Paperbacks
P.O. Box 227, Mankato, Minnesota 56002
Creative Education and Creative Paperbacks are imprints of
The Creative Company
www.thecreativecompany.us

Design by Blue Design
Art direction by Tom Morgan

Images by Getty Images/Annabelle Chih/Bloomberg, 62, CFOTO, 61, Chip Somodevilla, 67, David Paul Morris/Bloomberg, 30, I-HWA CHENG, 74, Jim Dyson, 51, Justin Sullivan, 34–35, Marlena Sloss/Bloomberg, 6, MediaNews Group/The Mercury News, 39, Rebecca Noble/Bloomberg, 48, Tayfun Coskun/Anadolu, 26; Pexels/Nana Dua, cover; Unsplash/Daniel Alexander, 73, Timo Volz, 14; Wikimedia Commons/André Karwath aka Aka, 24, Brett Samuel, 68–69, Coolcaesar, 22, FritzchensFritz, 29, Gary Halvorson, Oregon State Archives, 18, Gene Wang, 56, Jawed, 21, Martijn Boer, 4–5, 52, Peter Dasilva, 8, Prime Minister's Office, 12, Pronoia, 11, public domain, 58, The White House, 44, Presidential Palace, 2

Library of Congress Cataloging-in-Publication Data
Names: Silver, Erin, 1980- author
Title: Nvidia / Erin Silver.
Description: Mankato, Minnesota : Creative Education and Creative Paperbacks, [2026] | Series: Odysseys in business | Includes bibliographical references and index. | Audience: Ages 12-15 | Audience: Grades 7-9 | Summary: "Learn how Nvidia revolutionized gaming and AI through groundbreaking graphics technology. A perfect guide for high-school tech enthusiasts and creators shaping tomorrow's digital landscape. This title includes sidebars, a glossary, selected bibliography, websites, and an index"— Provided by publisher.
Identifiers: LCCN 2025021230 (print) | LCCN 2025021231 (ebook) | ISBN 9798895811368 library binding | ISBN 9798896800897 paperback | ISBN 9798895812624 ebook
Subjects: LCSH: NVIDIA Corporation--Juvenile literature | Integrated circuits industry--United States--Juvenile literature | Semiconductor industry—United States—Juvenile literature | Computer industry—United States—Juvenile literature
Classification: LCC HD9696.I584 N8575 2025 (print) | LCC HD9696.I584 (ebook) | DDC 338.4/762138150973--dc23/eng/20250523
LC record available at https://lccn.loc.gov/2025021230
LC ebook record available at https://lccn.loc.gov/2025021231

Printed in the United States

CONTENTS

Introduction

Nvidia founder and CEO Jensen Huang struts into a Denny's breakfast restaurant in East San Jose, California. Wearing his trademark black jeans, black t-shirt and black leather jacket, he slides into a booth for an interview. He feels comfortable in this setting. It was here where he washed dishes and bussed tables as a teenager and the exact location where he met

OPPOSITE: Jensen Huang's success story is a masterclass in resilience, innovation, and visionary leadership.

with his partners in 1992 to map out what is now one of the most successful companies in the world. Today, with Nvidia valued at over US $3 trillion, Jensen has himself become a billionaire by revolutionizing the tech industry with his AI microchips. These chips have made things like self-driving cars, facial recognition and text generation a reality.

At breakfast, Jensen orders seven items, including a a chicken-fried steak and pancakes, which he wraps around a sausage. "In the future, everything

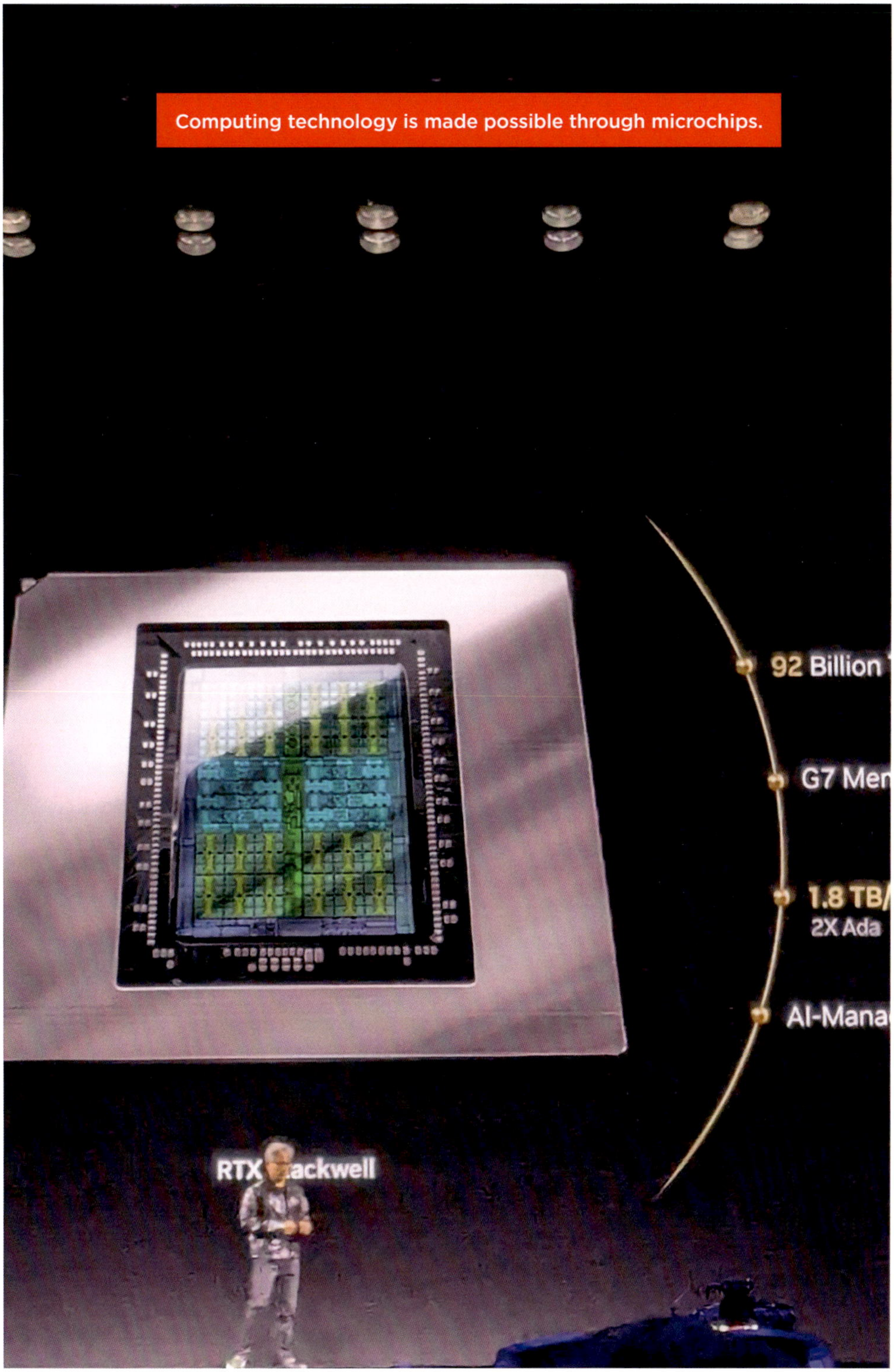

Computing technology is made possible through microchips.

Huang now meets with important officials across the world

that moves will be autonomous," Jensen tells the interviewer. He envisions robots fading into the background, much like microwaves and ovens, quietly taking over everyday tasks such as cooking dinner and cleaning up afterwards. Yet, as inspiring as his journey is, it has not come without risks. Jensen has faced moments when the company nearly went bankrupt. "I do everything I can not to go out of business," he admits. "I do everything I can not to fail." After the interview, Jensen accepts a plaque from the CEO of Denny's and leaves the server a $1,000 tip. Now, it's back to work for Jensen and there's no time to waste. The world is waiting to see what he'll think of next.

From busboy to CEO

Jensen Huang was born in Taiwan in 1963. He lived in Taiwan and Thailand as a child, but his parents wanted Jensen and his older brother to have more opportunity. When Jensen was nine, his parents sent him and his brother to live with an uncle in Tacoma, Washington, and then later to the Oneida Baptist Institute in Kentucky—but the school turned out not to be the respected boarding

OPPOSITE: Taipei, capital of Taiwan.

school they expected; instead, it was a reform academy for troubled youth. It was such a rough place that Jensen's roommate had even been stabbed several times in fights.

"Every student smoked, and I think I was the only boy at the school without a pocketknife," Jensen said.

Too young to attend school there, he walked to a nearby public school, where Jensen, with his heavy accent and long hair, was picked on and called a "Chink." "We were called that every day," he remembered.

By high school, Jensen's parents immigrated to the United States, and the family lived together in Beaverton, Oregon, where Jensen attended Aloha High School. Not only was Jensen a great ping pong player, but he was also a member of the math, science, and computer clubs. By age 15, he had a part-time job at a local Denny's restaurant. "I was a dishwasher, I was a busboy, I waited tables," he said. "No one can carry more coffee cups than I can." The breakfast chain would come to hold a special place in Jensen's heart in the years ahead.

At age 16, Jensen graduated from high school. Then it was off to study electrical engineering at Oregon State University. In a class of mostly men, there were roughly three women. One of them—his lab partner Lori Mills—caught Jensen's eye. But Jensen didn't think he

Oregon State University

had much of a chance with Lori. "I was the youngest kid in the class," he said. "I looked like I was about twelve."

Jensen didn't give up. "I tried to impress her—not with my looks, of course, but with my strong capability to complete homework." After about six months of doing homework together, Jensen asked Lori on a date. The rest is history. Lori and Jensen were married in 1985 and the couple moved to **Silicon Valley**, California to work as microchip designers. Jensen worked at **semiconductor** companies Advanced Micro Devices (AMD) and LSI

Logic and earned his master's degree in electrical engineering at Stanford University at night. Meanwhile, Lori took time off to have their two children, Spencer and Madison.

Sensing an opportunity, in 1992, Jensen sat down at a booth at Denny's diner in Silicon Valley with his two friends, fellow microchip designers Chris Malachowsky and Curtis Priem. "It had all the coffee you could drink, and no one would chase you out."

Stanford University

First-job advice

Jensen Huang has some advice for teens: "Start your first job in the restaurant business," he said. It teaches humility, hard work and hospitality. Jensen says that working at a busy restaurant taught him how to think calmly under pressure. It's also where he figured out his favourite way to eat pancakes—he wraps them around a sausage for pigs in a blanket. A plaque that reads "The Booth That Launched A $1 Trillion Company" now hangs over the booth where he and his co-founders met to discuss their plans for Nvidia. Entrepreneurs are invited to follow in Jensen's footsetps: Denny's hosts a Trillion-Dollar Incubator Contest, an award for creators of the best idea that originated in a Denny's restaurant.

Over cups of bottomless coffees, the three engineers mapped out an idea for a microchip that would create more realistic 3D graphics on personal computers. Jensen liked video games and thought his company could change the way video games were played. Though they originally wanted to call the company "NVision" they realized it already belonged to a toilet paper manufacturer. Instead, they named it "Nvidia" based on the Latin word invidia, meaning envy. That's because they wanted their competitors, companies like Intel and AMD, to be green with envy when they saw what Nvidia would accomplish. They even used the color green for their logo. In 1993, Nvidia was officially born. At 30 years old—and the youngest among the founding

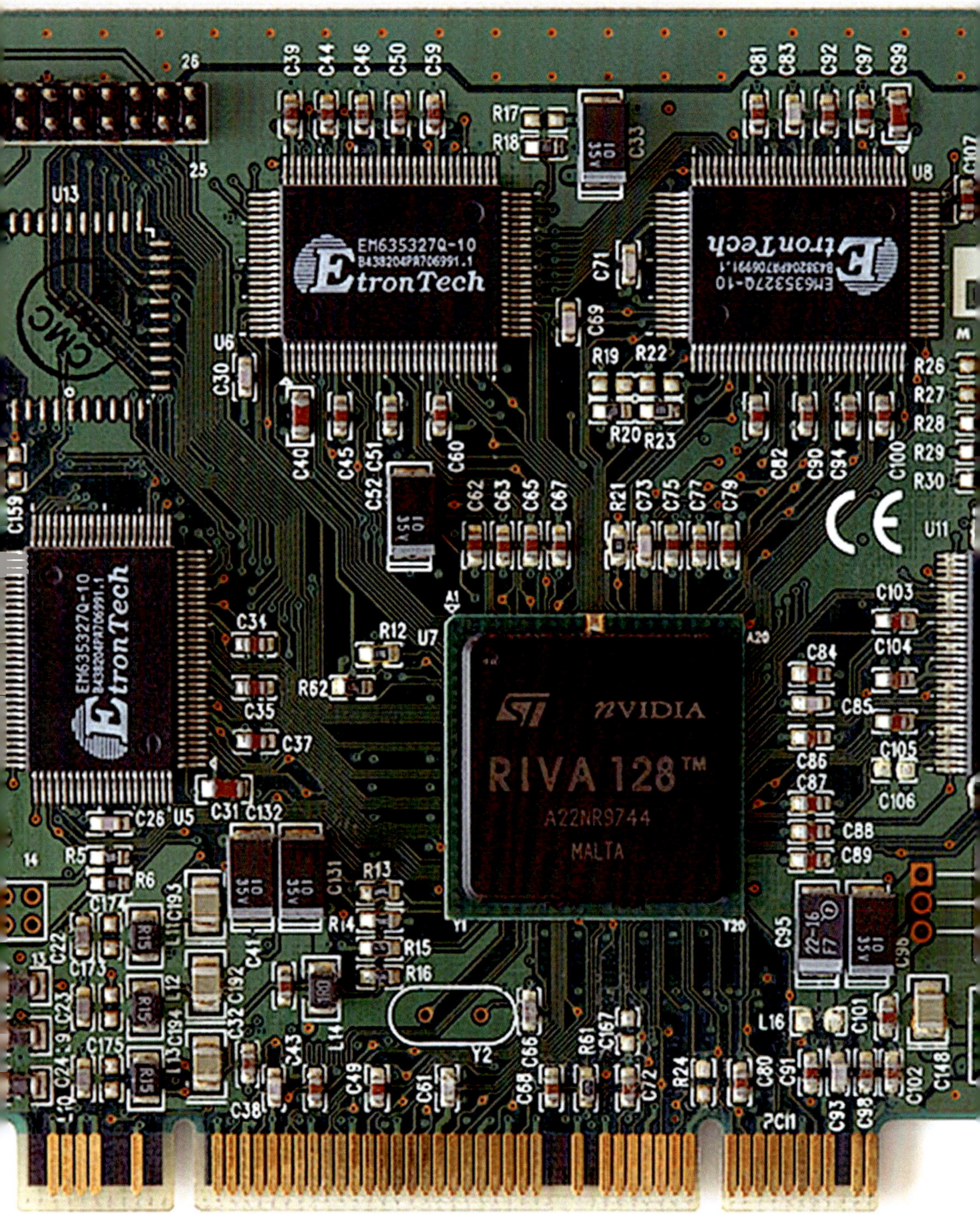

The Riva 128

team—Jensen was unanimously agreed upon as the best candidate to be CEO.

The company got off to a rocky start. Their first chip was a complete failure and didn't work with graphics software made by companies like Microsoft. Low on funds in 1996, Jensen laid off staff and started producing a whole new chip called Riva 128. "It was fifty-fifty," Jensen said of the potential success of the product, "but we were going out of business anyway." The company sold their Riva 128 chips, but they still only had enough

The importance of failure

Nvidia's headquarters in Santa Clara, California, features two striking buildings built in a triangular form. The triangle motif is seen indoors as well, appearing on everything from couches and carpets to even the washrooms. In Nvidia's early days, rendering triangles was essential for creating 3D graphics. In an effort to innovate, the company chose a different approach—rendering quadratic surfaces instead. Without the conventional use of triangles, the resulting chip failed, nearly sending the company to bankruptcy until a crucial pivot was made. Today, the triangle serves as a symbol of adversity, grit, and humility among Nvidia employees. "A reminder that we got it very wrong in the past, but we learned," explained one Nvidia executive.

money to cover a month's worth of expenses. "We were running on fumes," said Jensen. The idea that he was always 30 days from going out of business motivated him to keep innovating and working hard.

In 1999, Nvidia became a **public company** and released a new invention that would transform video games and the tech industry: a **graphics processing unit (GPU)** called GeForce. Unlike **central processing units**, which process information sequentially, GPUs can handle multiple calculations simultaneously—a technique known as **parallel computing**. This enabled video game graphics to have 3-D characters, better lighting, textures and high frame rates. Nobody had seen anything like it. Competitors started creating their own GPUs, and Jensen had to think fast. When his team realized that GPUs could do even more than create better video game graphics for systems like Xbox and PlayStation—like accurately identify images and recognize human speech—Jensen wondered, "What else can you teach it?"

By 2012, Jensen had an answer: artificial intelligence (AI). Though AI didn't really exist at the time, Nvidia realized the chips could be used for supercomputing—making the high-performance computers needed to run AI programs. Suddenly, Jensen had a vision. "He sent out an e-mail on Friday evening saying everything is going to deep learning, and that we were no longer a graphics company," said Greg Estes, a vice-president at Nvidia. "By Monday morning, we were an AI company. Literally, it was that fast."

At first nobody other than scientists and researchers knew what to do with high-performance computers. But then, everything changed...

NVIDIA GRID G
1080p 60 fp

From Games to Greatness

Nvidia's groundbreaking GPU chips changed the future of video games and turned the company's fortunes around. Combined with its **CUDA** parallel computing platform, created in 2006, users were amazed by how much more computers could do with its GPU chips—things like AI, deep learning, scientific modeling and more.

OPPOSITE: Nvidia chips have allowed videogame developers to push their games to higher levels.

Rather than solely celebrating the company's success with video games, Jensen chose to pivot. Although it was a risky move, in 2012 Jensen decided that Nvidia would focus on developing the hardware and software for a supercomputer powered by its GPUs. It would be used for more than video games—way more.

"We invented this capability and then one day the researchers that were creating deep learning discovered this **architecture**—it turns out the architecture was perfect for AI," Jensen told *60 Minutes.*

When Jensen talks about deep learning, it sounds like science fiction. But as he explains it, "Deep learning is a method. It's a new way of developing software."

At the time, even Nvidia deep learning researchers had doubts about AI. Researchers had tried to use it in the past, but they made little progress, and they gave up. "I didn't want him to fall into the same trap that the AI industry has had in the past," a Nvidia researcher said. "But, ten years plus down the road, he was right."

Jensen has been called a visionary for good reason. In 2016, Jensen hand-delivered the first-of-its kind Nvidia supercomputer to Elon Musk, who was then a board member at a company called OpenAI, a research lab that was developing ways to use AI. Using a black marker, Jensen signed the supercomputer with the

A 2024 Nvidia conference highlighted new chip, software, and AI processor technology.

words, "To Elon and the OpenAI Team: To the Future of Computing."

Within a few years, in November 2022, OpenAI launched ChatGPT—a **chatbot** that uses AI to answer questions, write content, and solve problems in a way that's similar to what humans can do. It can even translate information into other languages, write essays, stories, and social media posts, and solve math problems. The program had great potential to change how the world's companies could do business. And all these AI applications required Nvidia's technology to power it.

Meanwhile, people were already relying on Nvidia chips thanks to the COVID-19 pandemic. When the pandemic hit in 2020, people were stuck at home. Suddenly, the world's major economies depended on **data centers** and **cloud computing** to work from home, host video conferences and stream entertainment. Nvidia was in the perfect position: all of these activities needed Nvidia chips. And the company could charge more for their product. By then, Nvidia had an advantage over other chip makers. As the company that had invented GPUs, it had already developed better hardware and software, and its chips were more readily available.

All of these factors meant that Nvidia had cornered the market—it was the main supplier for companies that needed major amounts of computing power to manage their businesses and their AI needs.

That's when Nvidia really took off. Its stock prices soared and by May 2023, the company was suddenly valued at $1 trillion. By the next year, it was worth $3 trillion. Nvidia has far surpassed its rivals, becoming the most valuable semiconductor company in the world. It's even been called the "dominant" force behind the AI sector and "the most important company of the AI era."

In an instant, Jensen became a Silicon Valley superstar and his net worth skyrocketed to $125 billion. His 3.5 percent stake in the company made him the 11th richest person in the world. Jensen still isn't used to

Family matters

Two of the hard-working employees at Nvidia are Jensen's children, Madison and Spencer. Madison is Director of Product Marketing at Nvidia. She earned her MBA at the London Business School and also has a passion for food and wine. Colleagues call her a "top notch all star" who is "always willing to listen to new ideas" and is "an unstoppable force in the world of marketing." Spencer is a senior product manager who works with robots. While he used to own a bar in Taiwan, he also has an MBA from New York University and many more degrees and certifications in things like AI, human-computer interaction and Mandarin.

being a tech celebrity. He considers himself an introvert and still gets nervous when he speaks at conferences and appears at events like the annual Consumer Electronics Show in Las Vegas. He's amazed that people want to hear him talk, take his photo and get his autograph.

"It is the most extraordinary thing that a normal dishwasher-busboy could grow up to be this," Jensen said. "There's no magic. It's just 61 years of hard work every single day."

Jensen is a workhorse—and he demands the same of his staff. He's been called a perfectionist, demanding, intense and not easy to work for. But Jensen takes it as a compliment. "It should be like that. If you want to do extraordinary things, it shouldn't be easy."

At the same time, he's also called irreplaceable, brilliant, humble and even entertaining. He encourages his team to experiment with products that don't even have a market yet. And he also wants staff to learn from their failures. He has them make "failure presentations" where they analyze the steps that were taken, the decisions that were made, and the things that didn't work out so they can figure out what went wrong and course-correct. Jensen knows everything that's going on at the company and asks for weekly updates from everyone. He's also known for sending out hundreds of emails a day. He wants people to work "at the speed of light." In other words, find ways to be as efficient as possible—just like a computer. Working at Nvidia isn't the right fit for everyone. Yet those who stay believe in Nvidia's mission to advance AI. Many employees end up staying for a long time. Some employees are now so wealthy they don't need a job, but they still come to the triangular-shaped buildings to work every day.

Today, more than 40,000 companies use Nvidia AI technologies. These companies include the big ones like Amazon, Google, Meta, Microsoft and Tesla. Nvidia's

A Great Investment

Nvidia went from an unknown stock at just $4 a share to the leader of the AI boom—and its stock prices have leaped accordingly. For instance, those who happened to have invested $1,000 in Nvidia in 2014 would have made 321,459.94 by 2024. A $1,000 investment in 2019 would have been worth $29,378.39 in 2024. And those who invested $1,000 in 2023 would have earned $3,470.10 in just one year. Stock watchers are betting the stock is a good long-term investment, leaving more room for the company to grow and innovate in the years ahead.

chips are used in everything from **virtual reality (VR)** gaming and self-driving cars, to social media platforms, virtual assistants like Siri and Alexa and facial recognition for security at airports. They're also used in the world of cryptocurrency, in finance trading, to research and discover new life-saving drugs, to create lifelike sets and special effects in movies and to run advanced robotics.

And this is only the start of what's to come. "We are one year into generative AI," Jensen said in early 2024. "My guess is we are literally into the first year of

Jensen Huang speaks during an “Investing in America” event

"MY GUESS IS WE ARE LITERALLY INTO THE FIRST YEAR OF A 10-YEAR CYCLE OF SPREADING THIS TECHNOLOGY INTO EVERY SINGLE INDUSTRY."

a 10-year cycle of spreading this technology into every single industry."

Unfortunately, not every day on the job has been fun for Jensen. He's faced many challenges and controversies that still have the potential to make or break the company.

Facing fears head on

Jensen and his team at Nvidia have achieved great success, yet some factors remain outside the company's control. One issue that impacts all American semiconductor companies is government regulations.

In recent years, the U.S. government has limited how many advanced chips from companies like Nvidia and AMD can be sent to other countries. These chips are so important for things like security, the military, and intelligence that the government doesn't want certain countries to have them. These rules can change at any time. At one point, the most advanced chips were restricted from being sold to more than 40 countries across the Middle East, Africa and Asia to prevent them from ending up in China. Without being allowed to sell to these other countries, Nvidia's profit goes down.

This situation has spurred Chinese companies to rapidly develop their own AI technologies. Stock watchers were concerned when a new Chinese company, called DeepSeek, unveiled a new AI app in 2025. The DeepSeek AI Assistant took two months to develop, cost less than $6 million to build and outperformed OpenAI's ChatGPT. It's model was called "one of the

TSMC in Arizona

most amazing and impressive breakthroughs" one financial expert had ever seen. DeepSeek's app jumped to the top of the charts on Apple's app store and Nvidia stock immediately fell by more than 12 percent. If Chinese technology companies are able to provide more accurate AI at a fraction of the cost of American technology, how will American companies like Nvidia succeed in the future? It's a big worry for all American tech companies.

Another big worry is the fact that Nvidia chips are manufactured at a special facility in Taiwan. While Nvidia designs the chips, tests them, markets them and supports its customers, all the chips are made overseas by a company called the Taiwan Semiconductor Manufacturing Company (TSMC). It manufactures chips for other companies, like AMD, as well. If China takes over Taiwan, like it has threatened to do, the whole industry will be in trouble and the U.S. might lose its access to chips. As a result, starting in 2025, TSMC has been producing some of Nvidia's high-performing chips at a new manufacturing plant in Arizona. The plant cost tens of billions of dollars to build, since making these chips requires a highly specialized process. If one slight thing goes wrong, it could cost companies millions of dollars, if not more. While Apple and AMD are also turning to this new American plant to have some of their chips made, they would still need to be packaged in Taiwan. In the years ahead, it's expected America will need to rely more and more on its own resources to produce AI chips.

Jensen isn't afraid of challenges. He has overcome adversity many times in the past. In 2011, for instance, Nvidia and Intel were in a major legal battle. They managed to settle their law suits against one another

A Hard Day's Night

Musicians are increasingly expressing concern about the impact of AI on creative ownership. They worry that artificial intelligence could strip artists of control over their own work. "You get young guys, girls, coming up, and they write a beautiful song, and they don't own it, and they don't have anything to do with it. And anyone who wants can just rip it off," Paul McCartney, a former Beatle, told the BBC in 2025. "The truth is, the money's going somewhere. When it gets on the streaming platforms, somebody is getting it, and it should be the person who created it. It shouldn't be some tech giant somewhere," he said. Consequently, artists—from writers and musicians to other creative professionals—are calling on governments to enforce stronger copyright protections to ensure creators receive proper credit and compensation.

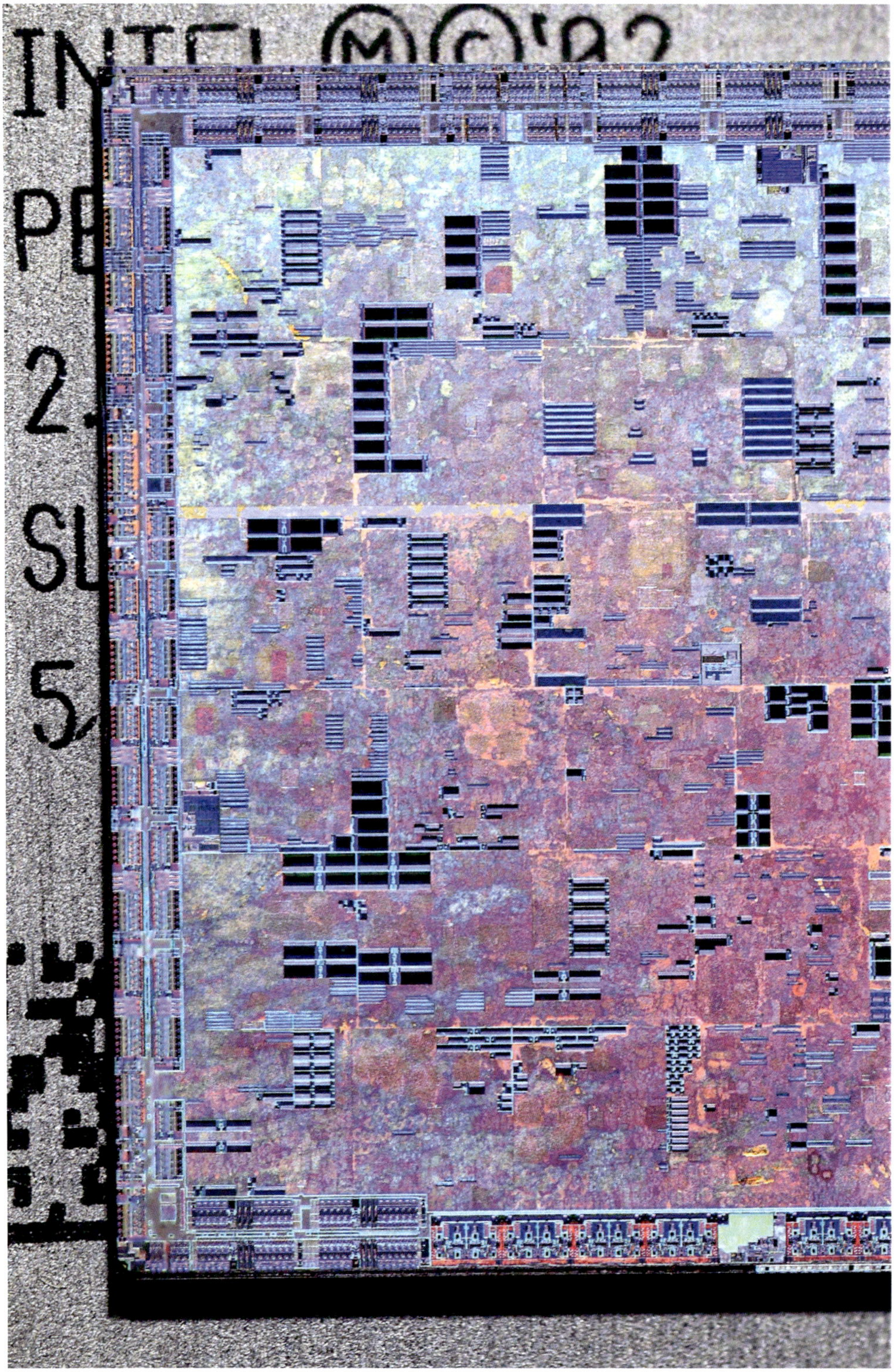

over the licensing of its technology. Intel agreed to pay Nvidia $1.5 billion and got to use Nvidia's technology in some of its chips. In exchange, Nvidia got to use some of Intel's technology to develop more of its own products. Jensen called the agreement a "new era for Nvidia" that "reflects the substantial value of our visual and parallel computing technologies."

Though he puts a positive spin on developments, things don't always go Jensen's way. In early 2022, Nvidia announced that a big deal with a UK-based chip designer called ARM was dead. Financial regulators ruled that if Nvidia bought ARM, Nvidia would have an unfair advantage over other companies. This could reduce competition, compromise product quality and innovation, limit consumer choice, and drive up prices. Though Nvidia promised it would share ARM technology with competitors, it was no use; government regulators said no to the deal. Nevertheless, in a press release, Jensen wrote in a statement, "ARM has a bright future, and we'll continue to support them as a proud licensee for decades to come."

Also in 2022, Nvidia faced a cybersecurity attack in which hackers stole the email addresses and passwords of 71,000 individuals, including Nvidia employees. The attackers used the stolen information to access internal systems and exfiltrate sensitive data.

When Nvidia refused the hackers' demand to unlock its chips for **cryptocurrency mining**, the group posted company data online. Nvidia quickly responded by advising affected parties to change their passwords, contacting law enforcement, and employing cybersecurity experts to secure its network. Luckily, the damage was limited.

Perhaps one of the most daunting challenges Jensen faces is public fear. Jensen remains passionately optimistic about AI's potential to drive medical breakthroughs, tackle climate change, and create safer vehicles. Yet many are skeptical of the technology. Concerns abound that AI could displace human workers, spread misinformation, or even be misused by terrorists to develop biological weapons. In 2023, dozens of AI researchers voiced their concerns to the government, sparking a collective movement to ensure that AI research could continue safely

Cousin rivalry

Nvidia and AMD have been fierce competitors for years. But Nvidia has come out on top. One report showed that AMD had 12 percent of the GPU market share while Nvidia has 88 percent, which means more businesses use Nvidia chips than AMD's. Interestingly, the CEO of AMD, Lisa Su, is Jensen's first cousin once removed. She is the second most successful CEO of a semiconductor company after Jensen. Though the two didn't meet until they were adults, Jensen said of Lisa, "She's terrific." While the folks at AMD think they can catch up to Nvidia, Jensen isn't worried about his cousin's company. "We're not very competitive," he said.

while preventing the spread of technologies that might be used for harm. Later that year, the Center for AI Safety released a statement—endorsed by 600 experts and public figures—warning of potential risks such as "extinction," "pandemics," and "nuclear war." Headlines following the release cautioned that the later stages of AI development could be "disastrous" and even lead to extinction; however, Jensen chose not to sign the letter.

While much needs to be worked out as AI advances, Jensen is an AI optimist. He believes that AI will simply make faster calculations to help humans solve problems and meet the world's challenges. He believes the future will be about progress and prosperity, not one where robots rule the world.

From sci-fi to reality

The future is uncertain, but anything is possible. AI is already capable of doing so many things in every day life. It can take a voice command to create a slideshow, turn a sketch into a website, or even summarize a book. AI can even score well on standardized tests.

"Twenty years ago, all this was science fiction," said Jensen. "Today, we're living it."

OPPOSITE: AI generation allow users to create images based purely on their imagination.

In the future, experts believe AI will manage investments, fly drones, create medicines tailored to each person's condition, serve as the brains inside robots, or even recreate the voices of people who have died. Experts look to Nvidia to make it happen.

Jensen is excited about the future—especially about the **metaverse**. Nvidia describes the metaverse as "the next era in graphics." It will be home to "connected virtual worlds and **digital twins**," including "digital human **avatars**." As Jensen explained it, "The combination of AI and computer graphics will power the metaverse, the next evolution of the internet."

Nvidia created a new platform, called the Omniverse Avatar Cloud Engine (ACE), that will be used to create and teach billions of digital human avatars to move and speak like humans.These avatars will be

DIGITAL TWINS
H-B
全息

A Nvidia employee demonstrates an AI-based character creator.

used as digital assistants that interact with humans, play online games and work in customer service at online stores. Using Nvidia technology, they are being taught to think and reason, and to help humans perform their jobs better. What kind of job can an AI assistant perform? They will help design chips, work with software engineers and market products. The process has already begun.

In addition to developing more advanced GPUs, Nvidia continues to study the hardware and software needed to create robots capable of operating in factories and warehouses, as well as building products such as phones, computers, cars, and planes. All this physical work will be automated by humanoid robots or even robotic arms. Humans will be able to communicate with these robots so that products will come off the lines faster and with fewer issues. These robots will even be able to solve problems.

"If this seems hard to imagine, consider that Nvidia has already produced technology that many people have seen without realizing it. Called **neural graphics**, it enables artists to create 3-D worlds and lifelike animation in movies—movies that can be made faster and with less money. Check out animated movies like *Cars, Monsters Inc*. and *Toy Story*—Pixar Animation Studios has used Nvidia technology to create these and many more of its movies.

In addition, anyone who has bought furniture, clothes or makeup online may already be using **augmented reality**. This is when online customers get to put new furniture in their virtual living room or see how they would look with a certain color of lipstick before they purchase it. This is thanks to new 3-D internet capabilities. It's changing the way companies sell their products and how people buy them.

If this sounds frivolous, the same technology can help with more serious tasks. In fact, neural graphics have enabled scientists to create a digital twin of the Earth to model climate change trends in the future. These models help experts create policies and technologies that may slow global warming and save lives. They also show the consequences of what might happen if no changes are made to how humans live and the kinds of energy they use. Just think about the natural disasters—things like hurricanes, flooding and wildfires--that humans wish they didn't have to face.

In fact, Nvidia is passionate about combating climate change. Already, Nvidia-powered AI technology is helping farmers reduce how much water they need for crops. It's helping factories reduce waste and be more energy efficient. And it helps shipping companies plan more efficient routes to reduce emissions. Companies that use Nvidia GPUs to dramatically speed up their work are 20 times more energy efficient than those that use traditional CPUs. More and more companies are adopting Nvidia GPUs to cut their energy consumption. Nvidia is also focussing on packaging, making sure that their products are shipped using material that is 100 percent recycled. They are also looking at their processes and measuring their **carbon footprint**, or the impact they have on their

Jensen-isms

Jensen is an in-demand speaker at university commencement addresses. Students always want to know how they can replicate Jensen's success. Here's some of his best advice, or "Jensen-isms:"

"If we don't build it, they can't come."

"Greatness comes from character, and character isn't formed out of smart people—it's formed out of people who suffered."

"What will you create? Whatever it is, run after it like we did. Run, don't walk."

"My first wish is for you to find joy in work or just fall in love with whatever work you do...That's the only way you're going to do exquisite work."

U9
U11
U10
NVIDIA
1274T00B30 0428A1
S TAIWAN
GEFORCE 6800 GT

U12
LB13
TP1
R95
R92

planet. Their goal is to keep improving and doing their part for the planet.

Nvidia is also committed to being a great place to work and to hiring individuals from diverse backgrounds. They established a program called Nvidia Ignite, to prepare first- and second-year college students for summer internships. Recruiters help women and members of the Black/African American and Hispanic/Latino communities through the interview process. They also offer flexibiltiy, so that current employees can work from anywhere in the world, in the Silicon Valley office or at home. As Jensen said, "The way I think about it is I'm investing in the next generation, to help us and to inspire us to create even better and more useful technologies."

Employees also do a lot of good in return. The company encourages staff to get involved in their communities. With a program called Inspire 365, they can have time off to volunteer and pitch-in to help good causes. Over the years, Nvidia and its employees have contributed millions of dollars and tens of thousands of volunteer hours to support everything from humanitarian relief, food security and environmental conservation to education and animal welfare. They also offer opportunities for staff to help tutor and mentor underserved communities and underrepresented students. Their goal is to help students succeed in math, science and reading and be introduced to AI. As a result of all these efforts, surveys conducted by Nvidia show that nearly 100% of employees are proud to work at the company and say it's a great place to work.

For his part, Jensen is generous as well. He donated $5 million to Oregon Health & Science University in 2008. In 2009, he gifted Oregon State University $2.5 million and $30 million to Stanford University in 2010. Through it all, Jensen has never forgotten where he came from. In 2019, he gave $2 million to build Huang Hall, a new

Nvidia's podcast

Want the inside scoop on everything from the future AI to how AI is helping the planet? Then tune into Nvidia's very own podcast, called the AI Podcast. It has already produced more than 200 episodes, which have been listened to more than six million times since the show launched in 2016. The podcast is a great way to learn how AI is shaping the world. Some of its most popular episodes include topics like AI in the classroom, how AI can help humans heal and AI's potential in the world of science. It's available for listening on virtually every podcast platform.

Jensen Huang (C) applauds during Computex 2025

classroom and a girls' dormitory at Oneida Baptist Institute where he lived as a boy.

Jensen has received numerous awards, including the Robert N. Noyce Award (the highest honor from the Semiconductor Industry Association), the Dr. Morris Chang Exemplary Leadership Award, and the Charles F. Jenkins Lifetime Achievement Award. In 2019, he was named *Harvard Business Review's* best-performing CEO.

Jensen has also been inducted into the U.S. Immigrant Entrepreneur Hall of Fame and was named *Fortune's* Businessperson of the Year multiple times and *Time's* 100 most influential people, in 2021 and 2024.

Now in his 60s, and the longest running tech CEO in the world today, Jensen is far from retiring. "I think it's fun to be inventing the next computer era. It's fun to see all these amazing applications being created." Jensen is often asked to speak and give advice. What are his best words of wisdom? "I hope you believe in something—something unconventional, something unexplored," he said. "You may find your generative A.I. You may find your Nvidia."

Selected Bibliography

Amara, Phil and Chin, Oliver, *More Awesome Asian Americans: 20 Citizens Who Energized America*, Immedium, San Francisco, CA 2022

Nvidia's Booming A.I. Business Collides With U.S.-Chinese Tensions. The chipmaker expects more than $10 billion in foreign sales this year, but the Biden administration is advancing rules that could curb that growth. https://www.nytimes.com/2024/12/19/technology/nvidia-chip-sales-us-china.html?searchResultPosition=6

The Furious Contest to Unseat Nvidia as King of A.I. Chip, Amazon, Advanced Micro Devices and several start-ups are beginning to offer credible alternatives to Nvidia's chips, especially for a phase of A.I. development known as "inferencing." *NY Times* https://www.nytimes.com/2024/12/03/technology/nvidia-ai-chips.html?searchResultPosition=8

The Next Robot Invasion, NY Times Jan 14 2025 https://www.nytimes.com/card/2025/01/14/business/2025-ces?searchResultPosition=9

Glossary

AI microchips special chips that can process large amounts of data at the same time and help with AI tasks

architecture the structure of a computer system

augmented reality an interactive experience that uses computer-generated information to create a world that looks like reality

Artificial Intelligence a field of study that creates machines and programs that can perform tasks that usually require human intelligence

avatar a figure that represents a person

carbon footprint the impact a person or company has on the planet

central processing units (CPUs) the main component of a computer that helps perform tasks

chatbot a computer program that's similar to having a conversation with human users,

cloud computing using a network of remote servers on the internet to store, manage and process information

CUDA Stands for Compute Unified Device Architecture and is a software platform and programming model Nvidia developed so developers could use graphics processing units (GPUs) to speed up computer applications

cybersecurity attack
when hackers illegally gain access to a computer system or network through the internet

data centers a facility companies use to house their important online information

deep learning a way of using AI to teache computers to process data in a way inspired by the human brain

digital twins a virtual replica that can be used in simulations

facial recognition a type of AI that uses a person's face to verify their identity

GPU Graphics Processing Units were invented by Nvidia and is a chip that can speed up image processing and make images look better. They are used in devices like video game systems, mobile phones and personal computers.

high frame rates a way of viewing images so it looks clearer and more immersive

metaverse the next generation of the internet that combines AI and computer graphics

mine cryptocurrencies
using specialized computers to calculate difficult math problems to make transactions with digital money

neural graphics a set of tools that lets artists create and animate 3D objects and worlds

parallel computing
a way of processing information at the same time

public company a company whose shares are traded on the stock exchange

self-driving cars cars that have the capability of driving themselves thanks to the help of AI software programs and other operating information used by a computer to complete tasks

semiconductor essential components of most electronic circuits used to run computers

Silicon Valley the area of California where many big companies including tech startups have their headquarters

supercomputing the fastest computers in the world used to solve complex problems

text generation when an AI system produces written content as though a human wrote it

virtual reality a computer-generated simulation that feels real

Websites

Meet Nvidia CEO Jensen Huang

60 Minutes, CBS, https://www.cbsnews.com/news/meet-nvida-ceo-jensen-huang-company-powering-ai-today-60-minutes-transcript/

This is a great short video about Jensen Huang, the man behind the company powering today's artificial intelligence.

Nvidia's AI Podcast,

https://blogs.nvidia.com/ai-podcast/

This is a great resource that includes interviews with experts on a range of AI topics, produced by Nvidia.

CES 2025: AI Advancing at 'Incredible Pace,'

NVIDIA CEO Says: Jensen Huang unveils NVIDIA Cosmos, Blackwell RTX 50 Series GPUs and AI tools for PCs.https://blogs.nvidia.com/blog/ces-2025-jensen-huang/

This page contains cool videos on all the latest things Nvidia has been working on.

Index